Some
of us

and most
of you

are dead

Other Titles by Peter Norman

At the Gates of the Theme Park
Emberton
The Gun That Starts the Race
Water Damage

Some
of us
and most
of you
are dead

Peter
Norman

A Buckrider Book

Buckrider Books is an imprint of Wolsak and Wynn Publishers.

Cover and interior design: LOKI
Author photograph: Melanie Little
Typeset in Lyon by Kai Bernau, Commercial Type
Printed by Coach House Printing Company Toronto, Canada
Cover and interior images are found photographs, Monastiraki, Montreal

The publisher gratefully acknowledges the support of the Canada Council for the Arts, the Ontario Arts Council and the Government of Canada.

Buckrider Books
280 James Street North
Hamilton, ON
Canada L8R 2L3

Library and Archives Canada Cataloguing in Publication

Norman, Peter, 1973-, author
    Some of us and most of you are dead / Peter Norman.

Poems.
ISBN 978-1-928088-68-4 (softcover)

    I. Title.

PS8627.O76S66 2018   C811'.6   C2018-903872-1

Contents

To Me
You were
Invisible

Sorry for your wounds. To me you were invisible.
The night was sick with fog. Plus, my headlights
flicker sometimes. All I saw was hooves
kicking at my windscreen, and you slipped
away between columns of pine. We let ourselves
drive blind. We trust the feeble light above.
With gun and illness, reel and rod and saw,
we tell ourselves we have subdued a continent.
Some of us and most of you are dead.

Last Cubed
Inch

Today I surfed on a clod of lava.
Today I tried to pass as someone else.
Today I fucked, gestated and broke water,
birthed a pouch of skin containing no one.

Wasted day. Not like the time I climbed into a boab,
carved my query on its inner skin.
Or when I posed as midwife, birthing others'
offspring, filling tiny fists with weaponry.

Better to ponder what tomorrow holds:
A three-ring rave. Tent fire at the circus.
Leeches latched upon a swimming swami.
The lighting of the last cubed inch of tallow.

I nag: *Little no one, make me a grandmother.*
I'm pregnant again, but sonar shows only stones
I swallowed in a bout of dudgeon;
entrails arrayed for *I Ching*
divination. Swallowed pits. Rusted blades of grudges.

Out of My
Element

The diving board is miles high. The pool is fathoms deep.
I slice my neck to make the gills of the fish I need to be.

Entropy is fate. I've seen the future and am stricken.
As grand as ancient godheads were, as fickle, as
destructive, still the tide will nullify their names.

This is the pool I tumbled seven centuries to die in,
this the goggle-sporting rogue whose fiat
I obeyed, still clueless of the fish I was to be.

Poolful of wildweed. Flummoxed, I wildered,
champing bladderwrack, ducking under
kelpine polyps chundered endwise.

Up my rectum sensed a cosmic boot.
Time to climb. I wriggled up a
rope of bubbles in the aqua null.

What pump-inflated bauble do I rise to?
Bursting, what comprises protobang?
What prole dross chase I, sad quotid-I?

Chlorine pierces me; I seep an *ah*.
I don't exactly come but something comes
from me, shades from *maybe* into *is*.
Inhaling cradling pool, I float beholden.

If the Pressure
on Our Hearts is
Adequate

I'm at your door. The welcome mat is frayed.
Clouds thicken, flicking tongues of lightning.
Storms down power lines throughout the central
counties; news reports show farmers nailing boards
to cover windowpanes. This can't be good.
I've stood in one too many haunted halls
sheltering while someone gets a coat. Trees
crackle with impending charge. A genuine
conundrum swirls above; the darkness wheels,
cavorts. Advancing storms are measured
by the atmospheric pressure, how it hurts
barometers' couched hearts. Last April
pressured hard and – do excuse my language –
preparations weren't so fucking adequate;
the county let us down again. A budding
bramble heaves and sighs. I will contrive
to bundle you out here into my truck,
where we will ride the rhythm of the engine
throbbing in our seatbacks as we idle,
talking small, and secretly we'll measure if at all
the pressure on our hearts is adequate. You'll fly
away to somewhere distant for a year,
cocoon yourself in education. Stars
will keep their vigil over tended fields.
We who stayed will shamble through our lives
as pressure systems gather in the ether.

Out
Late

Manic beats accelerate the dance.
Midnight's fallen; all spells are complete,
the phantom carriage morphed into a riddle –
vegetation sprouting wheels – wind
whistling in the glassy sole, coachmen riding
helplessly to unsprung traps. Come for a spin
around the floor. My waltz is barely worth
a splinter of the burnished wood
it batters. My body is a hollow
gourd, its pulp and seed the mirth
that turns to fury in a zealot's gut.
Beware the eye's preliminary twinkle –
arpeggios upon the devil's fiddle.

Common Etiquette
for Standing
on Holy Ground

Forgive the father. He was drunk;
his homily was rank with not-so-wisely chosen
curses. A lapse, not a crack-up.
Withdraw your phones; deactivate the cameras.
Don't be crass. This is a sacred place.

Take off your hats. Be humble. Mull the bullets
plucked from martyrs' ribs at autopsies
and sealed in glass. Butcher all the verses of
the printed hymn. Eternity will not be compromised
by your extortions. Godhead-flesh has melted

in our mouths, in wafer form. Kneel, dogs,
conceal that cleavage. Ixnay on your dodgy
and "creative" prayers, you so-called artists.
The Popemobile was cross-hatched by a key.
Libertines like you sent martyrs to their deaths.

It's been a rough millennium. The whole shebang's gone
south. We've read the testimonials
and wept. We've sat unmoving through the pitch
of every schizoid Christ. The True Lord sits on high,
but soon he'll be back down. Judgment's coming with.

Begone. We're here for those who shredded knees
on our half-thousand steps. We've alms to waste on beasts
who gulp the meal and jabber. Surplices to launder;
surplus cash to launder too. Upgrades to the wireless
and the weapons. Paint job on the papal car.

I Know I Am
(or, Think Basic)

Say what you will about the times when joy caved in to rage.
Say what you will, but know: I'm not oblivial.

Sure, I stew. But then I force my brain to buck the toxin and
      ascend azure,
cloud-spattered heights and hover dronelike. This is chief
      among my talents,

those that still exist unburied. Necklaces of birdlife rise and flow
in fond formation to my waiting hand.

Should you arrive up here, shout out. I'll take you on a tour
and show you the ionospheres that banish even colour.

Cirrus fringes will engulf your contours,
ozone patches preen and stretch to flaunt their range of tint

until each quad's devoid of sides. So long, oblong.
Float with me until we tire and plummet, dumbbells

'roid-rage deities let drop. Grounded now, I stew. I eye cashiers,
aye, aye; yes, ma'am; no prob – the slipshod verbal

simulacrum of that stultified, elusive
peace we see in venerated paintings.

I will admit, my brain is base. My toenails are divine.
My inner organs? Their conditions vary.

Of course, the liver is a toiling dynamo
whose only recompense is to outlive us –

yes, I believe its taut, pocked, med-gown-green
exterior will be adored in some anatomizing studio

where interns make incisions, climb astride
the disembowelled remnants of a stranger or a stranger

form of humanoid. My liver's plump with pilfered
    diamonds,
the chambers of my heart with indecision.

Say what you like. Do as the parrot does
and croak at every pet-shop chump: *I know I am,*
    but what are you?

Spree of Second
Deaths

Diurnal slog. Triumphs ever fewer.
Garbled edges of palimpsest proofs
proving nothing. I work so cheaply
I should pay these wages back to you.
(Cue the violins.)
Today has waned. Don't know how I spent
the bulk of it.

Why can I not sit still?
I chisel out a line occasionally.
Sidle off, get busy washing
stubborn stains from fabric. Walk the dog, her
hackles rigid as we near a suburb
wandered by unresting spectres, blurs against
the ranks of polished picture windows.
The shadow on the sundial barely moves
even when I watch and scream at it.

Bundled poems into mourning suits,
sent them downslope on a broken sled. Carry
your freight with pride but do it shyly.
The most expensive vase again stands empty.
I had sophisticated drinks, the finest meals,
bonded with my shadow over whisky.
Scrawled condolences in greeting cards,
pocketed inherited medallions.

A dripping faucet no one fixes.
Blinds that slant and simply won't come down,
the slats of which resist all forms of washing.
Dust gathers to a maelstrom under sofas or
assembles on the page. Dust breeds anywhere.
If I could siphon all the dust and sculpt it, I could
shape a saga to subsume you.
Carry your maximum load, but shyly:
safety first. The future is the children,
pure as not-yet-fallen snow,
shriekingly oblivious of what they hurtle to.

Grabbed my rifle, hunted spectres. Got 'em all, a
spree of second deaths. Felt the night's first gale dressed
in snowflakes, drifting, laughing, pulling
into perfidy toboggans and their wads of literature.

Gut-Blade
Gospel

Yes, I consent to tote your cross
although in sin we are not equals.

I'm broke as hell, but here's a quarter.
You're the better man by half

or by infinity. I read in red the words you say,
your speech to those who will not hear.

Netted fishes wriggle at your question.
Gut-blades answer with a slash.

Twelve
Anguished
Men

Christ spoke. I listened. I'm not sure how true
his words were. Tough advice on giving alms.
The motley bunch onshore dispersed. I set the jib
and he and I and the eleven bailed. *What ails*
you, Master? Judas whinged. A mermaid, armless,
flopped on deck and bitched about her thyroid.
Our Lord and Saviour healed her with sibilance
as we alleged disciples yawned and napped –
until he bagged from barren seas a sturgeon
twice his size. Along his godlike mug
I marked a fortnight's growth of manly bristles.
Jesus threw the fish back in, ever the jester.
Render unto Caesar. Then he crushed a gnat
that landed on his holey palm. Poor bug. Such luck.

Heartbeat Muffled by a Vest of Virgin Wool

Long talks chockablock with moth
clichés and *hell, let's have another glass*
and bloviating experts in their fields
chewing chaff extracted from the wheat
their fathers' fathers grew. Smoking jackets,
tarnished pocket watches, squat top hats,
marbles in the toes of their big boots,
they chat about debarnacling their boats.
Supple words from a long tongue split
and coated with a layer of black earth
and healed/hardened by a weekend on the sea.
Gentlemen, goodnight. Conversers rise
and bow and chortle, fold their feathered wings.

Who is this grinning dimwit I've become?
What stubby twig was drawn
determining that I should pass
my days like this, instead of baling hay
or commandeering steer with coils of rope
or hefting vats of smelt as mournful whistles
herd my comrades in and out the gate?

Ma said there's a role that each man plays.
Ma made soup from shards of bone
and flecks of meat she'd labelled *My Mistakes.*
She chided me for the pursuit of thrill
and found the wadded notes
jammed in my pockets, written to the air.

Son, she said, *my dove, that's it.*
I knew your filthy mind was somewhere
else. You owe me. Pony
up. It's time you find some other place
to live. Time you change your name.
I acquiesced. I left that shack and stopped
so much as thinking about her.
On hostel bunks, I stroked myself and sang.

Self-made man. And *hell, another glass,*
let's hail the waitress back. My heartbeat's
muffled by a vest of virgin wool.
More chat about the markets. Chat of this
and that with old, fat fingers drumming
on the gleaming tabletop. I jam my smallest
digits in the caverns of my ears.

Obsessive
Convulsive

Tremors began no sooner we'd arrived.
Tremors in the ground on which the holy sites
were clustered; tremors in the profane streets
and pleasure-garden paths;
shudders in the graveyard stones
and judders in the beggar's empty tin.

Touring designated wonders,
meticulous appeals to a god
who rarely cared, I trembled like an athlete
overtaxed. I fluttered in the breast
and ululated in the trachea.
As if to blur the violence I'd seen,
my ocular equipment quaked, and earth
in counterbalance shook. My sex, however,
only grew more rigid. Somehow lust
was roused by all the quaking, gorged on it.

Ornaments toppled in our rented room.
Scrabble games were shattered, fallen letter
clattering on fallen letter. Old pornography
became dislodged, scattered in the attics,
slipped through windows to resume its work.

The quake persisted, rumbling on and on.
We waited for a break. We waited years.
We couldn't leave; planes declined to land there,
ships to dock – the hostile ground forbade them.
We hunkered in our prison, shaking one and all,
until the tremors were a form of gesture,
until we started to regard them
with tolerance that ripened into love,
and spasm was accepted as caress.

Crushed in Slow
Motion

Brandishing a twig, she wrote my name
on sand gone clammy with foam.
It's not a good ledger, she fretted, *the beach.*
Words come undone like a sloppy stitch
under the pressuring hand of the sea.
She placed a pressuring hand on her eye.
Its ache wouldn't ebb. *I think I'm being*
crushed in slow motion. A song
by rollers is wrung from my flesh.
Soon I'll be music and ash.

She scanned what she'd written. *Your name*
is no secret, but where are you from?
That's your riddle. I wasn't equipped
with an answer, and burning, I crept
to the grass-fingered fringe of the beach and escaped
from the tide of her voice, and the me it might sculpt.

Do What You Feel
We Feel You
Want

Loitering with crew & co.,
doing as the alpha does
or doing what you feel we feel
you want. Getting laid in a manger,
getting quarts of sense
knocked from your head. Who doesn't
crave the big-ass novelty check
given by grinning suit-'n'-tie men
as PR bulbs go off? But charges always
mount. The check goes through, but damn, the cash
     don't last.

Aphrodisiac
Catechism

That evening we scarfed oyster-flesh to excess,
lifted cloth to dab our lips with,
hoped this grub would get us lucky.
Lucky. That's what parlance claims it is
to wrestle, garmentless and sleepless,
under a naked sky or in a room
strewn with souvenirs of love,
artifacts of bygone pas de deux;
to moan or squeal or snort,
smash the hourglass, disperse the sands
until their blizzard pocks the neighbours' eardrums.
Oyster juice makes tendrils on our cheeks. The catechism
we recite but can't quite learn
by heart is painted on the wall. Excuse yourself
and slip from bed and read it. *God bless you,*
I intone, wishing God the Father were awake.

Resurrection
in Ash

I and an old foe fought beneath a rotted tree.
Not all rotted: one branch lived; a last, bleak leaf
jutted from it in a hopeful pose.
Otherwise the tree was black and fully void
of life. In its shade, we battled in the mud.

This was out behind the factory.
Barbed wire guarded aqueducts;
flies gathered at the stinking moats
and in the shadows under bridges,
having journeyed from the marshes,
slid past predatory birds,
stopped to posit eggs in sewage pipes.

We wrestled as a cyclone made of birds
tore through slate-grey cloud. The world
had long ago been stripped of "seasons";
"rain" was ash, as if each night the dead
were gathered and rescattered, sure as clockwork.

I had her in a headlock when the sparrows –
hunger-mad, mistaking us for insects –
plunged, began to peck. Tiny scarlet holes,
rash-like, blossomed on our skin. The dismal yard
was freckled with our blood. Little more than grains of wheat,
bits of her and me were tweezed in beaks and eaten.

I saw my foe bleed from her spiracles.
I saw my own blood steaming in the daylight.
My sword went slick and limp. The spear she held
had snapped. Beaks plumbed the purple fissures
in her neck. I saw my own flesh split
in one long seam, and hers a grid of notches.

And then, as one, they rose: the avian masses
winged away to savage fallen apples
at the factory farm. I stood, reset my stance –
but she was open-mouthed and pointing where the solid
scum had split, and ashen figures clambered from the moat...

Excavation
of the
Pointless

He said there was work to be done on the heart.
Clusters of bramble to clear from its groves.
(Let's not be insipid and claim old loves
squatted there, menacing peace.
They have no lease.) He made a start
with a scalpel that will never cease
to carve me in my earned unrest –
carved his monogram upon my breast,
pried free the hoarded joys.
He tweezed a pebble from my core.
I keep it in a mason jar, right here,
suspended in acidic equipoise.
It has no meaning anymore.
It's pointless, like any old sphere.

Scoured
Shore

Waves lick rock and turn it dark.
Gulls ride updrafts, cruising wrack-strewn
shoals for shells to crack. The whole shore's scoured.

No fauna speck's exempt – some adversary wants
its meat. Kelp-heaps teem with savage
clots of life, mite-swarm scaling

scales in decay. New swells punch
a lichen-scarred expanse, heave up to lift
flotsam offerings to bulging middens.

A gull attains its killing height, lets go the shell,
tilts inquisitor's head to watch,
dives down before its feast is drawn back under.

*

In a gash of tide pool seen
by you alone, a shadow snaking
after flecks of feed

gets thwarted, swarmed
by rival minnows, drags
its length to a wedge of unlit water.

Its blackness shows a red incision
something nasty slashed, a lesion washed
in salt – it stings, but better that than air,

the cruellest element. The creature's halfway dead:
you can discern the pulsing of its terror,
tremor in the hide, just barely there.

✳

Seal to salmon, grebe to crab to worm,
the food chain shudders with the surf. Claw stabs,
beak rends, dashed shell cracks with gun-

shot efficacy, gull-cry rises
over wind and crashing chop,
slices air before it's blown

by gale out of hearing. Mussels drop
and shatter, half their innards gone to waste
as birds fill up, fly off. The salt-licked world

staggers into twilight. Immanently still,
the length of shadow waits, enacts a part
written for it long ago. Shrinks from you who kneel

and peer. Exerts invisibility, its only art.

Cyanide
Sequel

Pinned and labelled, what presumes to move?
What motion is permitted in the glare
cast through a magnifying glass? We'd prove
in time that time creates the dance. The fury
smouldered hotter as we stoked it, and the skill
that we acquired and flexed was never stranger
than a fly, fixed in amber, drawing thrilled
hurrahs by spreading wings. Bright with danger,
aloft on our applause, implausible spectres
brushed the crypt's ceiling with unseeable wings,
flung back our faces in reflectors
that were, in fact, their eyes. Listening
to shimmers in the air, did we go blind
as music made its chrysalis in our mind?

Nothing
Like

Eyes like vulture wingspan or ama-
tory dirge from lusty keeners keeping
frost awake in lovely woods. Nothing
comes of noting single grains of sand.
A crowd of one cannot attempt the wave.
Your tree of quills is blotting out my window,
feathered like the gaudy caps you'll
don when daybreak terminates the dream.

Tonight we dim the lights for atmosphere,
dull our thinking for the sake of seance,
make like we don't see the medium's feints.
Black wires criss-cross one another.
Power can't escape the current circle.
Metaphors are pinioned on a slab.

Through a Portal
Darkly

Is it a crime I strive to be more beautiful
than you? Sorry, hon, this Pinot's
not my cup of tea. Let's not traffic
in these luxuries I end up pissing
out an hour later in the fishtank.

Forgive me, dear, we're here to talk of you.
You dazzled when you entered that first door
but underwhelmed in later portals. You committed
"crimes" against our "taste," but that's okay and
kind of sexy too. Let's focus on particulars:

you had alluring lips and brutal credit;
exuded charm in runnels when you felt like
charm was called for; sashayed boldly with
the muscled baddies; strutted up the middle
of the runway you'd been kicked from yet again.

This Bordeaux's brutish. Let's not play at "nice";
even pretending, you can't be that cute.
Hike your skirt; I'll shrug aside my jacket.
This rented bed's a ledger for our leavings,
even after maids' discreet adjustments.

We met in a summer storm in a stormy city
under the din of a rain-hammered scaffold.
You greeted me; I said some shit like *Word*,
back then a useful word that opened doors.
Whatever you were offering, I wanted it.

You let me in your door, fantastically.
Fortune can befall the fool who badgers
even as it scorns the one who hears
the dogged offer. Anyway, we bent
our bodies into puzzles past cerebral,

stoked our furnaces and lay there telling
lies to keep the light alive. Brute me,
uncouth and ragged me, going by feel,
lonely earwig on a picnic dish,
untutored in the etiquette of ants.

We thought: equality. We scored as lateral
the passes past. We thought the storm out there
was where the rupture showed. Was where the
hurt came from. But knowing's always virtual.
We knew fuck all, my dearest. Word. That's life.

The Agitation
Game

Totting emphases. Tongue math.
Agitation of the elements;
periodic fizzing up
of sentiment or sediment. The testing toes
Narcissus dipped in water. Toaster
slit receiving fork. The shock absorber trade.
I once was lost but now am found.
Lord, lead me lost again.

Graffiti but with antique paint.
Squeal of soles of ballers swivelling.
The murmurs of the figures in the dumpster there,
wrapped in castoffs, talking wrong,
rummaging subsistence from our waste:
their current is our surest currency.

Cleanse without Compromise

A face inscribed by its own cleansing:
long scar showing where a slide
did as it must and hastened down;
grooves a glacier scraped.

Apocalypse of rock
shedding scabs. Apocalypse of ice.
Points and edges mellowed by the filing.
Pumice face made glossy by the polishing.

Tell me I'm wrong to want that cold,
relentless element to make me shiny.
Say it can't be right to prize that granite
flesh – fresh, clean garment, cut down to my size.

Cannibal

Many species cram the fridge.
It's hideous how tight
I've jammed these creatures
in. I may have broken laws.

Some are curled like shrimp,
some splay arms like octopi
or puff to prominence their gutted husks
and cling in single-minded clumps.

They won't be sold for any price.
Who'd pay? Replicas, erected in squares,
made me something of a star
fish – I was gifted three new arms

laden with ravenous suckers
impossible to pluck by hand.
I mapped my body with exactitude;
biologists derided me for this.

Sometimes fluid was discharged
allegedly imbued with sex.
Appetite enclosed me whole,
dribbled from redundant arms.

Time to sober up. Felt the master's lash.
Sold my extra limbs and bought a cello,
scraped a keening murmur
worthy of my victims' doleful gaze.

Parts of me are loaded in that fridge
and garlanded with flora from the sea.
I core the strands of DNA for data,
find myself predictably awash

with swill you'd find in any random beast.
I take a sample on my dripping tongue.
This feast is base. No way to make it noble:
me the cannibal, exhuming victim me.

Natural
Red 4

Cast-off bug-skins dust the unwashed sill
and cling in spectral clusters to the screen
and to a hopeful ear are noted singing
ballads of the freed bug, which elsewhere sings

dashing its voice against a frigid breeze
beating song-fists upon a rigid chest
within which nothing lives or pumps
and all's damp grey, there is no flash of ruby

anywhere, yet for a lurching moment
lustful microbes may perceive a spark
inside the hollow chamber – but the day
is mortal, and the daydream's wings are gone.

Help
Me Up

Help me up. I'm sucking air.
I'm sucking overall. I cower in a closet
jammed with stench, unpalatable

as a senile uncle with his fly left open
and self-awareness gone real small,
shrunk to the length of a micro-micro-second.

The past has failed to set me up for this
invincible explosion of domestic dust.
The vacuum cleaner's fake, a jokey decoy

left by clowns to throw us for a loop.
Something's crooked. Funds have been diverted.
Security just lets the villains in.

You sitting down? I'll spill my secrets
seed by seed (they're seeds). I'll garnish them with
cartridges of spermicidal foam

and hand them over. Please don't tell the staff.
My walker's new and swish. It's wheeled
to help me push it fast and equalize

the rat race to the dining room, contested course
past doors a tad ajar and voices meant
to not be audible. This ain't what we agreed

to, years ago – but change, they tell us, is the only given.
Fine. I'll bow down to my better
and pray for his expiry in a fire.

I'm not long for this world. I know arithmetic;
I've done the math. Nature's pegged me an
avuncular redundancy. Senility itself.

Back in my day, we had excitement, music, movies.
Flung back neon drinks and gorged on popcorn,
posed and moued. But fade-out ended every movie.

Bearing Cross, in Seven Easy Steps

Collapse will happen later. First
we sag without quite falling down;
first we scrabble, gathering the change
the charitable hurl, the needles from a church
whose sense of aid is just a pinpoint off.
First the mattresses of upturned knives
we're laid on for the guards to laugh
as the bacillus tally mounts.

Guards will sneer. Don't answer them.
Don't voice your panic that you bleed all night;
keep no tabs on the terrific fee
nights wring from your flesh, your seeping rump.
Most of all don't pine for where you're from.
Don't recall a mercy-swaddled world;
nix faith that there's a somewhere suffering
is dimmed. Know only dark,
its agonies, its brute seduction. Merely care
for your endurance, here, with us.

Don't gouge away the branding from your forehead.
Don't flinch at what comes climbing from the pot
our meals are simmered in. Every moment's passing
means a horror's past. All things turn out,
at last, to be just what they were. No one
can sweeten that. Endure. Remember that your roaring
gains you nothing when we reach the end.

One Day of
This

The day's bereft of moments
worth a social post, worth blowing horns
or screaming *You are always*
fucking up or *Babe, don't burn that book.*

The day is out for blood no sooner it begins.
The day's designed to shred you with its angry
beaded whip. The day is other people,
and it's hell. A holding cell you will expire in.

The day is deaf to plaints that start *I need* –
The day will taunt you if you try *I want* –
The day's unmoved by your *I'm not okay.*
The Sun, to your *I'm dying*, answers, *Tell the hand.*

The face is ninety-three million miles away.
They said so in a documentary.

Rogue
Wave

Surf is mighty. I'm a puny swimmer.
Ocean rises and I raise a fist,
maybe dare to fling a bellow first.
Tsunamis never flinch. Their liquid grammar
bundles up the flotsam of my language,
wrecks the structures I erect. Each burst
shack's forced forth until it's braced
against a body stronger than the surge.

Surely every wave will be drawn back
into the bosom of the ocean that exhaled it?
Surely some accountant notes the lack
of edifices left, enacts an audit?
The wave retreats with everything I know,
which isn't much. I wilt and watch it go.

Chairman
in Crisis

Cosmos rarely comes of chaos.

The chairman flashing CanLit cufflinks tables
his amendment to the scansion table.
Undergrads carve hearts into the ceiling,
jam their gum on hallway oleographs.
The chairman teaches verse all day
to acolytes who'd rather learn each other.

They study prosody but dream of legs
enfolding them, discuss whom they would nail
if chance arose, betray their lust and malice
quietly through faux pas in the kitchen,
roll up sleeves, divulging old abuse.
The plump one, armoured in his beard, announces
that he carved ghazals on inner walls of eggs,
but no one's too excited by his news;
they shrug and turn attention back to poems
due tomorrow, due to blur all borders.

The chairman perches high upon a promontory,
gazes down like academe's devoutest scholar
scrutinizing annotated *Odyssey*s
and deconstructed *Iliad*s.
Down the cliff the sea becomes a mirror
showing him himself as Nureyev,
as equipoise personified in a performance
no one saw and yet the mirror caught.

Plush seats, a podium, a screen define the lecture room
where students dream decrepit barnyards,
heaps of shit-strewn hay where fallen godheads play
wrapped in skin they scavenge here,
cloak themselves in mere mortality:
swan's plumage; bumble's buzz;
feline stealth; tortoise longevity;
eagle's width before she folds and drops;
peacock straining to erect his wilted splendour.

The chairman wonders if he is a poet,
really, after all. He lets a frown
disturb his moistened forehead.
Just last week he coined a metaphor: a coffin
is the socket yearning for the excised eye.
Pleased, he jotted it along his palm
and later scrubbed his hands with bleak ferocity
and saw at once the sum of wasted years,
the scansion table no one reads, a marriage
Robert's Rules imposed, the times he had the floor
and rose to speak, and quailed, and just could not begin...

The Luxury
to Which You are
Entitled

Our most exclusive suite accommodates
a negative number of guests. With icicles
of steel, the acupuncturist rejuvenates
botulinum toxin in your brow. Certain cycles
of the tub exfoliate the mildew that accretes
in conscience never flexed. Swapping exuberance
for stylish tedium, point-one-percenters dance
to silent tracks on the onyx floor; its tile secretes
a truffle oil that repels the lonely.
Our genie is on call to grant the wish
of the guest who has no needs and only
craves the gift of loss. Don't turn squeamish
when the moment comes. Accept with grace
the whorl of blades advancing on your face.

Sugar Halo
Aftermath

Two trucks crash. An icing sugar
supernova haloes one. The other truck
exhales flour. All over town

sirens cry, and waiting bakeries
get news, and grieve. So many sweets denied us.
So much proxy love. It's February.

Markets beg for tarts and pastries, not for bread.
Road crews hose the asphalt, scatter empty sacks.

The 14th has a history. We don't remember
whose – the namesake's faded from our tales.
All we know is we are meant to get
the sweetness due, our teaspoon of attention.

Windblown crystals make obscuring curtains.
Medics rush to victims we can't see.

Lost Beyond
the Reach
of GPS

Up from the underground, I lose my way
to the ballpark. Workers watch,
silhouettes in tower windows,
casting bets over which way I'll go.
I hear the crowd roar before I get far,
but try as I might, I cannot find them.
Eyes ingest me through windows.

My phone has died. I've lost my way
and have no GPS. The lights are taking
far too long to change. Someone offers drugs
then shuffles off. I meet the eyes of workers leaving
offices, of crows and feral cats
and, draped in tarp, emaciated children.
Where's the stadium? The final game's today.

I never meant to come alone.
I had an extra ticket, asked some
friends. They all said no. Their children
had appointments, or they planned to go in groups
and watch from boxes, or to bring their child
and spouse. Everyone had someone else to be with.
Everyone had obligations, or lovers, or children.

What street is this? The final game's today.
I hear the fervent crowd and cross a road
I do not recognize. A passerby suggests we share
a joint. My hems are tugged by hungry children;
nothing I say or do gets rid of them.
I'm hounded now by crows and felines too,
swishing claws at me and at each other.

The crowd intensifies its cry. A faint moon
strains to be seen. Coast to coast, the country
is transfixed by this, the final game, and
those with means to buy a ticket will,
and anyone with eyes to watch it will.
I turn into a cul-de-sac, uncertain where I've come,
or even where it is that I came from.
The only certainty is eyes and windows.

Silent
Sentence

The face in the glass grips its cheeks in the manner
of a model for Munch's *The Scream*. Blue fire
flows from its eyes, drenching carpets.

What sentence has confined me to these rooms,
my only companion the wraith in the mirrors,
the one conversation I'm granted to hear
the whisper of moth wings aroused in the night,
the guttural surges of water in fountains
where algae amass in clusters the colour
of lung? Thus I atone for a lifetime of debt.

The living arrive. They stock up the cupboards,
kindle the fire, take rags to the quicksilver
sheen of the glass. I struggle to taint their reflection,
to rise draped with cobweb like Triton with seaweed
and blaze. But look at me. Meagre as vapour. My thin,
whimpered plaints dribble out, and the fools barely shiver.

Pre-nup
in a Precarious
Age

Muffle the clock. The cruelty of time
can go unheard. Don't struggle to be whole:
collect your fragments, sharpen them, take aim
and fling them with a modicum of style.
Dial down the heater; set the lamp to dim –
let's shiver in the twilight for a while.
Spew hostilities before you come.
Hide the ointment so the gall won't heal.
Let mildew colonize our cave
and filaments of gangrene bind my hand.
Set fire to the deck before you deal;
burn the scripture that instructs your soul.
Don't violate our oath by turning kind –
ensure the poison's never mixed with love.
Serve it straight, this medicine I crave.

The Will
to Outshriek
Everything

First hint of light, they snap awake and sing,
note by note, in mindless music-box
rotation. I'm awake as well. I'd rather be
sunk back into my dreams than up and thinking.

Dread hauls sheets aside, flicks on the lights,
betrays the piled butts and clustered empties.
The plant that I forgot to feed has lost its bloom.
Dust furs the silhouette of every artifact.
My failure slouches into light, and they are watching.

They chide. They explicate my sorry themes.
They chirp through almost any weather.
Their wit is undermined by fallacies,
their gravity by all the jokes they crack.
I cannot use my porch; they've claimed the railings.
I see them pluming from the far horizon,
plague of crop-consuming beetles
sent by deities as wrath or warning.

Reliable as autumn rains,
their favoured themes recur.
They scold me for the pain that I defer
and ask what all this pleasure-seeking's for.
I tip the bottle, but they sing till I pass out,
and when the dawn inserts its livid hook
into my eyes, they start their song again.

I'm no actor. I can live without an audience.
They scrutinize the flat where I'm contained.
Heads cock with judgment. *You are boring.*
Addicts are. Their judgment's infinite;
no coda to the carping symphony.
I long for smothering winter –
foliage gone, and song. I'll roam, a ghost let
from its attic, maunder in the gutter.

But winter's brief. Too soon the promised thaw
draws them out again with voice to spare,
with pent-up music; lungs that know
no reticence; the will to outshriek everything,
to sing a lesson no one else will teach,
regale me where I shudder under fleece,
breach the rubbled bunker of my sleep.

She Plays
the Femme Fatale,
but Who Plays
You?

She's a dab hand with unctions and jellies,
the residue a nasty patina
legible along your cracking lip.

Her skill is undisputed, but her art's not safe;
its glutted victims, rank and sated,
strew the anteroom, clutter the lounge.

Avoid the skewered snacks, the spiked champagne,
the vial of "good stuff" hauled from a sleek jet purse;
decline the invite to a "private show."

Or not. No need to fear the coroner;
he'll wait. Accept the open canister.
To the breathless question, whisper back: *I do.*

Poisoner /
Victim

The poisoner's hands are long and beautiful.
He crumples the verso page and smooths the recto.

The victim's throat has turned a soothing blue.
Blue mist billows in the cranial dome.

The poisoner's preferred career would be in clockworks
but sometimes in life, a dark door opens.

The victims are motley and mottled, cyan, ragtag.
Mute audience, they don't exhort he take his bow.

The poisoner can't do this anymore.
All he gets is guilt. Remuneration's nugatory.

Sometimes a voided victim will renew
her strength and twitch, then slip back to anonymous.

Poison can enliven for a time, inebriate.
Victims thus affected may ventriloquize.

A victim took the poisoner's voice one evening,
mumbled mumbo-jumbo, stilted hoo-haw.

The poison's in a vial on the glassed-in shelf, right there.
Want a swig? Go on. He says you're welcome.

First-Person
Prophet

I am the fury penned on the walls of the ward,
scarred into ceramic lake,
carved in lead-caked walls inside the ward,
notched on flesh to mark the crawling time,
hatcheted into the living pines.

Frothing, I forget what I was for.
The foam that brims my lip is flecked with green.
I drool and swell. A glutting largeness
splits me at the apex of the dream.

But I'll prevail. I am the edge sunk deeper
in your epidermis. I'm the sleeper
cell whose waking up negates the world.
I am the sequined lie the serpent told.

Evensong:
An Omen

Clothing smeared with chlorophyll and sand,
legs weary after bouts of Mother May
I, now we plump on soggy ground
and bicker (*Way. No way.*)
and pluck at blades and hope to pass
through boredom to the dinner call. A bird
falls near us, twitches on the grass,
makes vocables that nearly go unheard.
We gather at it, poke the broken wing. You stroke
the skull's peak till the bird goes calm
and silence wraps us in a suffocating cloak
so thick it's getting hard for us to see –
the twilight's vast and blinding, like eternity.
And then, at last, the call: *Come in. It's time.*

On Hearing
My Last Rites
Spoken Aloud

I could not, at first, be buried,
November's ground unbreakable. A veil
of silk ensnared my limbs, ensured I would lie still,
and still I lay when spring
softened cemetery earth. A shake
awakened me; my box was hoisted to the cold
outside the shed. I saw my veil unravel,
the coffin lid spring free and blazing arms
lift me to an agony of light –

Beneath the Neon
Galaxies,
We Dream of
Windows

Ceiling engineers assure us someday
drilling will be done and we'll see sunlight.
Meantime, sky is all inverted sod and light is
nighttime neon or diurnal halogen. Sanities
buckle as the cave endures. The planted
"surface flowers" wilt. Rank weeds assert
supremacy down here, a serpentine rebuke.

Deep in a ceiling crevasse, there's a door –
at twilight's cusp, or dawn's, or
anytime the system flickers, an abrupt
rectangle flashes there. Custodians at mowers
wrench their concentration from the "grass"
to view that geometric marvel neatly
tucked into the sky's hysteria.

Correction: not hysteria. We honour the profuse display
of dirt and rock and tip-of-root that is our mother sky.
We thank it for its gifts, the many vital things
it drips or drops or oozes to us, even for its faint,
pervasive death-scent. Even for its rages,
shudderings that send us clods to bruise
the pate – grace can strike the unprepared as vicious.

Beneath the neon galaxies, we dream of windows
onto vistas we could never worm up to –
such are the dreams of those of us born "under,"
limbs that spent a lifetime cased in plaster.
A tremble in the earth; another minor slide
showers us with root and rock. It's possible that glaciers
chew the world above, but nothing lives to notice.

Notices are posted by the planners
commanding we weed out conspirators
who mutter better caves are out there, unsurveyed;
who speak in coded whispers to each other,
gather ominous as huddled buzzards
(birds we know from myth and song and sketch).
We're safe, the planners state, within our borders.

But even the obedient crave open air.
In dreams, we clamber from our buried suburb,
up into corrosive rains and toxic, ashen snows.

Pronouncing
the Revelation

My palate problem's worsening.
My tongue has trouble formulating *ch*.
I can't say *please* or *do*. I can't say *me*.
I spill my noises on a rumpled bed.
I stutter: *m–m– n– sh– th–*,
bowling balls ejected from the mouth.
Interrogator: *Are you decent?* All I manage is a *no*,

moaned badly. Laces wink and slip their eyelets.
Drawstrings tighten at my throat. I'm toast.
My promises are ash. I killed the covenant.

The Oldest
Happy Ending
in the Book

Where the path divides, beside the stunted oak,
my brother grabbed his girl, told me to walk –
more exactly *take a hike* –
so I went off in search of snakes along the brook.
That's when the ground began to shake
and trees to groan. I wondered how much mayhem
    this would make
before the spell was broken and I woke –
the oldest happy ending in the book.
But no. This was the waking world. Into my own small Styx
I sunk one foot and then the other, waded out
to an old log, its bark a code of scuffs and nicks –
a behemoth too big to sink, too dead to float.
And then I spied them on the bank. The mad,
    contrary motion.
Earth spun. Trees writhed. The river gibbered ciphers
    to the moon.

Notes & Acknowledgements

Each poem in this book is a *terminal* – it borrows its line-ending words, in corresponding order, from another poem (for example, a terminal of "Roses are Red" would have to end line 1 with *red*, line 2 with *blue*, etc.). Appendix A lists my source poems and where I found them. Often I've tweaked the borrowed word (for example, in one case, *corner* becomes *coroner*); those changes are listed in Appendix B.

This project was supported by grants from the Canada Council for the Arts, the Toronto Arts Council and the Ontario Arts Council through its Works in Progress and Writers' Reserve programs. Some of the writing and revising was done during a 2015 residency at MacEwan University; thanks to the faculty, students and Edmontonians-at-large who made that happen, particularly Jacqueline Baker.

Versions of poems in this collection originally appeared in *Bywords*, *Contemporary Verse 2*, *Event*, *The Fiddlehead*, *The New Quarterly*, *ottawater* and *Peter F. Yacht Club*; thanks to the editors. "Aphrodisiac Catechism" (under the title "Stimulant") was an honourable mention for the John Newlove Poetry Award, judged by Gillian Sze.

Profound thanks to Paul Vermeersch for his brilliant editing, and for accepting this book into his Buckrider family. Thanks to Noelle Allen for giving the collection a home, Ashley Hisson for steering it through the stages of production, Emily Dockrill Jones for the superb copy edit and Kevin Yuen Kit Lo for designing a magnificent cover. Nothing I do, creative or otherwise, would be worthwhile without Melanie Little, who sustains me with her unflagging love and support. My final and deepest gratitude, as ever, goes to her.

Appendix A:
Source Poems

The Agitation Game, p. 42

Jeff Latosik, "Richard Hamilton's *Toaster*," in *Safely Home Pacific Western* (Fredericton: Goose Lane Editions, 2015).

Aphrodisiac Catechism, p. 32

Roo Borson, "Whuff," in *15 Canadian Poets × 3*, 4th edition, edited by Gary Geddes (Toronto: Oxford University Press, 2001).

Bearing Cross, in Seven Easy Steps, p. 49

Gil Adamson, "Chalk Cross," in *Ashland* (Toronto: ECW, 2003).

Beneath the Neon Galaxies, We Dream of Windows, p. 68

Margaret Atwood, "The City Planners," in *The Circle Game* (Toronto: House of Anansi, 1998).

Cannibal, p. 44

Peter Norman, "The Perfect Octopus," in *Water Damage* (Toronto: Mansfield Press, 2013).

Chairman in Crisis, p. 53

Irving Layton, "Greek Fly," in *Selected Poems 1945-89: A Wild Peculiar Joy*, expanded edition (Toronto: McClelland & Stewart, 1989).

Cleanse without Compromise, p. 43

Marilyn Dumont, "Guilt Is an Erosion," in *A Really Good Brown Girl* (London, ON: Brick Books, 1996).

Common Etiquette for Standing on Holy Ground, p. 18

Kevin Connolly, "History Channel," in *Drift* (Toronto: House of Anansi, 2005).

Crushed in Slow Motion, p. 30

George Elliott Clarke, "Elegy for Blair States," in *Black* (Kentville, NS: Gaspereau Press, 2007).

Cyanide Sequel, p. 38

Margaret Avison, "Butterfly Bones: Or Sonnet Against Sonnets," in *Selected Poems* (Toronto: Oxford University Press, 1991).

Do What You Feel We Feel You Want, p. 31

Nikki Reimer, "what makes you organized?" in *[sic]* (Calgary: Frontenac House, 2010).

Evensong: An Omen, p. 66

Archibald Lampman, "In Beechwood Cemetery," in *Selected Poems of Archibald Lampman* (Toronto: Ryerson Press, 1947).

Excavation of the Pointless, p. 35

Charles Sangster, "In the Forest," in *A Century of Canadian Sonnets,* edited by Lawrence J. Burpee (Toronto: Musson, 1910).

First-Person Prophet, p. 65

Gwendolyn MacEwen, "Dark Pines Under Water," in *The Selected Gwendolyn MacEwen* (Holstein, ON: Exile Editions, 2007).

Gut-Blade Gospel, p. 24

bp Nichol, "The Complete Works," in *As Elected* (Vancouver: Talonbooks, 1980).

Heartbeat Muffled by a Vest of Virgin Wool, p. 26

Lorna Crozier, "Small Resurrections," in *15 Canadian Poets × 3,* 4th edition, edited by Gary Geddes (Toronto: Oxford University Press, 2001).

Help Me Up, p. 47

Vincent Colistro, "Food," in *The Walrus* 11, no. 8 (October 2014), later published in *Late Victorians* (Montreal: Signal Editions, 2016) with different line breaks.

I Know I Am (or, Think Basic), p. 20

Christian Bök, "Voile," in *Eunoia* (Toronto:
Coach House Books, 2001).

If the Pressure on Our Hearts is Adequate, p. 16

Karen Solie, "Migration," in *Pigeon* (Toronto: House
of Anansi, 2009).

Last Cubed Inch, p. 14

Kerry-Lee Powell, "The Other Grandmother,"
in *Inheritance* (Windsor, ON: Biblioasis, 2014).

Lost Beyond the Reach of GPS, p. 57

Robyn Sarah, "Fugue," in *In Fine Form*, edited
by Kate Braid and Sandy Shreve (Vancouver: Raincoast
Books, 2005).

The Luxury to Which You are Entitled, p. 55

Eric Ormsby, "Hate," in *Time's Covenant: Selected Poems*
(Emeryville, ON: Biblioasis, 2007).

Natural Red 4, p. 46

Patrick Friesen, "The End of Things," in *A Dark Boat*
(Vancouver: Anvil Press, 2012).

Nothing Like, p. 39

Camille Martin, "Page Dust for Will" (first section), in
Touch the Donkey no. 1 (Ottawa: above/ground press, 2014).

Obsessive Convulsive, p. 28

A.F. Moritz, "Petra," in *The Sparrow: Selected Poems*
(Toronto: House of Anansi, 2018).

The Oldest Happy Ending in the Book, p. 71

Peter Van Toorn, "Mountain Stick," in *Mountain Tea*
(Montreal: Signal Editions, 2003).

On Hearing My Last Rites Spoken Aloud, p. 67

Leigh Nash, "Reincarnation," in *Goodbye, Ukulele*
(Toronto: Mansfield Press, 2010).

One Day of This, p. 51

Jacob McArthur Mooney, "Mark Coleman's Daughters Are Turning Out Okay," in *Don't Be Interesting* (Toronto: McClelland & Stewart, 2016).

Out Late, p. 17

Milton Acorn, "The Completion of the Fiddle (N.M.)," in *Jailbreaks: 99 Canadian Sonnets,* edited by Zachariah Wells (Emeryville, ON: Biblioasis, 2008).

Out of My Element, p. 15

Dennis Lee, "diggity," in *Testament* (Toronto: House of Anansi, 2012).

Poisoner / Victim, p. 64

Anne Compton, "The Provost Responds," in *Asking Questions Indoors and Out* (Markham, ON: Fitzhenry and Whiteside, 2009).

Pre-nup in a Precarious Age, p. 60

Steven Heighton, "Drunk Judgement," in *The Address Book* (Toronto: House of Anansi, 2004).

Pronouncing the Revelation, p. 70

Angela Carr, "of the worst," in *The Rose Concordance* (Toronto: BookThug, 2009).

Resurrection in Ash, p. 33

Meredith Quartermain, "Matter 24: Organography," in *Matter* (Toronto: BookThug, 2008).

Rogue Wave, p. 52

Joshua Trotter, "The Teacher and the Peach," in *Jailbreaks: 99 Canadian Sonnets,* edited by Zachariah Wells (Emeryville, ON: Biblioasis, 2008).

Scoured Shore, p. 36

Steven Price, "Field Guide to the Sanctuary," in *Omens in the Year of the Ox* (London, ON: Brick Books, 2012).

She Plays the Femme Fatale, but Who Plays You?, p. 63

Nyla Matuk, "Lust," in *Sumptuary Laws* (Montreal: Signal Editions, 2012).

Silent Sentence, p. 59

Anne Hébert, "Manor Life," in *Poems of French Canada*, translated & edited by F.R. Scott (Burnaby: Blackfish Press, 1977).

Spree of Second Deaths, p. 22

Erin Mouré, "Post-Modern Literature," in *The Green Word: Selected Poems* (Toronto: Oxford University Press, 1994).

Sugar Halo Aftermath, p. 56

Jen Currin, "Substance," in *The Ends* (Vancouver: Nomados, 2013).

Through a Portal Darkly, p. 40

Ken Babstock, "Second Life," in *Methodist Hatchet* (Toronto: House of Anansi, 2011).

Twelve Anguished Men, p. 25

Jeffery Donaldson, "A Touretter's Twelve-Tone Sonnet," in *Slack Action* (Erin, ON: Porcupine's Quill, 2013).

The Will to Outshriek Everything, p. 61

Helen Guri, "Doll Chorus" (the three poems by that title), in *Match* (Toronto: Coach House Books, 2011).

Appendix B: Changes to Line-Ending Words

Simple
Changes by
Category

Sixteen times, I took only the final syllable(s) of the source poem's word (e.g., *atmosphere* became *sphere*); four times, I absorbed the source word as the final syllable of my own (e.g., *it* became *audit*) · Eleven verbs were reconjugated · Seven plurals became singular or vice versa · Six simple homonyms replaced the source words (e.g., *sticks* became *Styx*) · Five times, a final *s* was dropped to change the category of the word (e.g., the verb *cloaks* became the noun *cloak*) · Four times, a possessive or contraction-forming apostrophe and/or *s* was deleted · One prefix was added (*decision* became *indecision*); two were dropped · One abbreviation replaced the full word (*company* became *co.*) · One adverb was stripped down to become an adjective (*infinitely* became *infinite*).

Other
Changes

The Agitation Game, p. 42

toast became *toes*

Aphrodisiac Catechism, p. 32

do became *deux*; *wakeful* became *awake*

Beneath the Neon Galaxies, We Dream of Windows, p. 68

Sunday became *someday*; *blizzard* became *buzzards*

Cannibal, p. 44

claws became *laws*; *Botticelli* became *bought a cello*

Cyanide Sequel, p. 38

safari became *fury*; *frill* became *thrilled*

Do What You Feel We Feel You Want, p. 31

manager became *manger*; *lists* became *last*

Evensong: An Omen, p. 66

sand became *sound*; *dismays* became *May*; *chime* became *calm*

Gut-Blade Gospel, p. 24

bp Nichol's "The Complete Works" replicates a typewriter keyboard; each line ends with the symbol found on the extreme right-hand key of the corresponding row on the keyboard. In "Gut-Blade Gospel," those symbols are rendered as words: the plus sign is *cross*; the equal sign is *equals*; the one-quarter fraction is *quarter*; the one-half is *half*; the quotation mark is *you say*; the apostrophe is *speech to those who cannot hear*; the question mark is *question*; the slash is *slash*.

Heartbeat Muffled by a Vest of Virgin Wool, p. 26

past became *pass*; *trill* became *thrill*

If the Pressure on Our Hearts is Adequate, p. 16

either became *ether*

Last Cubed Inch, p. 14

baobab became *boab*; *weapons* became *weaponry*; *swam* became *swami*; *chin* became *I Ching*

Lost Beyond the Reach of GPS, p. 57

rugs became *drugs*

Natural Red 4, p. 46

things became *sings*

Nothing Like, p. 39

panorama became *wingspan or ama-*; *capsule* became *caps you'll*; *scenes* became *seance*

The Oldest Happy Ending in the Book, p. 71

flout became *float*

Pre-nup in a Precarious Age, p. 60

Hell became *heal*

Pronouncing the Revelation, p. 70

convenience became *covenant*

Resurrection in Ash, p. 33

motive became *moat*

Scoured Shore, p. 36

rockstrewn became *wrack-strewn*; *sculling* became *scaling*; *worst* became *waste*

She Plays the Femme Fatale, but Who Plays You?, p. 63

satiety became *sated*

Spree of Second Deaths, p. 22

violence became *violins*; *Guatemala* became *got 'em all, a*

Sugar Halo Aftermath, p. 56

socks became *sacks*; *ponytails* became *tales*

Twelve Anguished Men, p. 25

napper became *napped*

The Will to Outshriek Everything, p. 61

fur became *for*; *teats* became *teach*; *sheep* became *sleep*

Peter Norman has published a novel and three previous
poetry collections. Born in Vancouver, he has lived in
Calgary, Edmonton, Windsor (Ontario), Ottawa,
Montreal, Halifax and Toronto, where he now lives with
his wife, author Melanie Little. He makes his living as a
freelance book editor.